Valentines Day Body Paint Chocolate Recipe Book For Couples - Perfect Valentine Recipes With Chocolate & Brush - A Naughty Gift For Holidays & Adults

Mary Kay Patterson

Published by InfinitYou, 2017.

All rights reserved. No part of this publication may be reproduced or transmitted in any form or by any means, electronic or mechanical, including photocopy, recording or any information storage and retrieval system, without prior permission in writing from the publisher.

© 2018 by InfinitYou

Introduction

How to Make No-MESS Naughty Homemade Chocolate Body Paint in 10 Minutes or Less!

If you are looking for a naughty Chocolate Body Paint Recipe you are on the right page.

This booklet includes a method to make some Naughty Chocolate Body Paint that is Guaranteed To Please your lover.

If you are truly looking for a very unique way to celebrate your love like an anniversary, St Valentine's day, or any other occasion that celebrates your love, this booklet is perfect for you.

Save money and do something really naughty with chocolate on that special day!

Ingredients * Directions * Tips * Licking the Spoon (and other utensils) * If you get Stuck * Gift Idea Resources * Some unforgettable & mentally challenging moment that you can experience with warm chocolate body paint + an iced chocolate martini!

Get started today and create the most unforgettable Chocolate Body Paint moments that you have ever experienced...

Naughty Chocolate Body Paint Recipe

If you want to surprise your man or woman, why not spice up your dessert time with some naughty chocolate body paint moments?

Chocolate body painting is a very delicious, naughty, sexy and stimulating way of celebrating an emotional time between lovers.

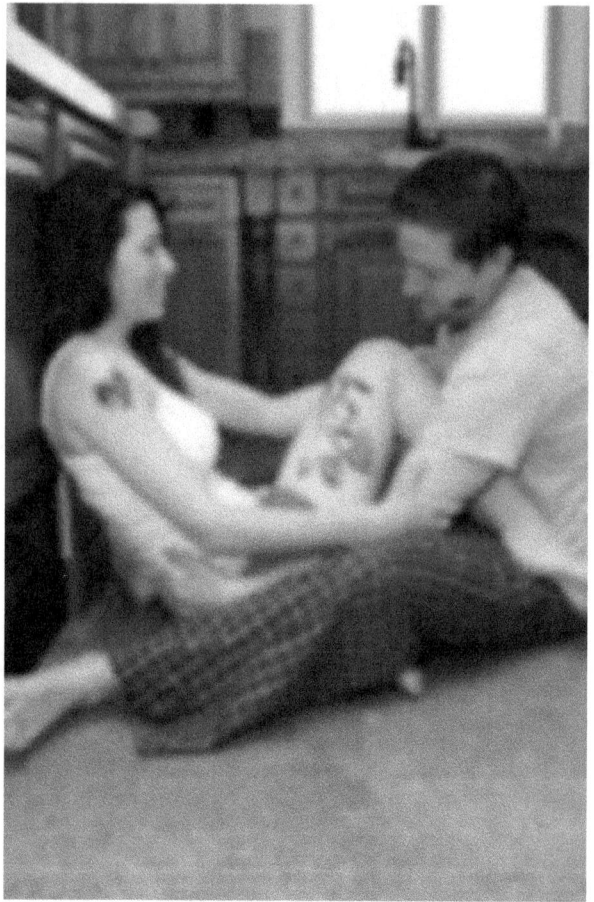

Ingredients For The Naughty Chocolate Body Painting Experience:
 2 tablespoons of high quality chocolate extract
 1/3 cup of granulated white sugar
 1 pinch of kosher salt
 3 tablespoons of source water
 2 tablespoons of chopped butter
 1/4 cup of good quality cocoa powder (because cocoa powder makes the difference)
 1/2 teaspoon of vanilla extract

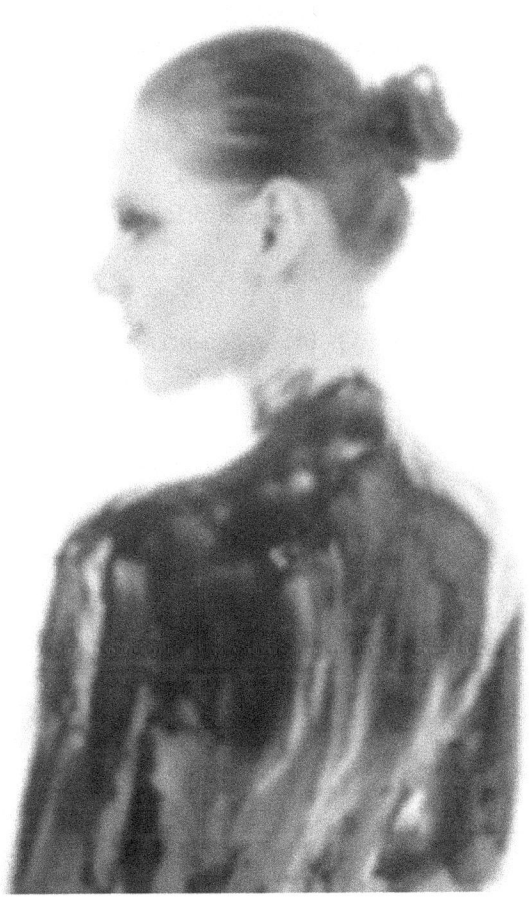

Directions:

First take a large saucepan and pour in the white sugar, the kosher salt, and the spring water.

Next heat your pan over medium heat until the mixture begins to boil.

Do not stir the mixture at all.

Once, the mixture begins to boil, keep lowering the heat of your oven and bring the mixture to a simmering state.

Once all the white sugar granules have dissolved in the mixture, remove the pan from the heat. Add the chopped butter and keep whisking until the butter is combined into the mixture.

Add the cocoa powder, the vanilla and the chocolate extract. If you are going to add some of your favorite alcoholic booze, now is the perfect time to add your favorite alcoholic beverage.

Next, whisk to combine the booze with your mixture.

The mixture may be lumpy at first sight. Do not worry about this.

Whisk until the mixture is totally smooth and looks velvet.

Next, test the mixture out with a wooden spoon.

If the mixture is prepared like above, you should get a nice thick coat.

Once the chocolate body paint has cooled down, but is still warm, you are ready to paint your bodies.

After a while, notice the chocolate body paint may thicken.

In this case, you can quickly reheat it in the microwave or you can use a double boiler.

You can also refrigerate the unused portions of the chocolate body paint in the refrigerator for future naughty moments.

I wish you a very naughty and sexy chocolate body painting experience!

If you are using the chocolate body paint as a gift proceed as follows:

Pour the still warm chocolate body paint into a decorative jar. Use the cafepress.com idea from below (section: some more naughty gift ideas) or find a decorative jar on sites like Amazon.com. You can also write or print your own label. Just use the internet for some inspiration what to say on your label. Search for search strings like "sexy inspirations", "naughty St valentine quotes", St valentine's day sexy lines", and so on.

Optional:

1/2 tablespoon of your favorite alcoholic booze. I love to use Baileys or some other Irish cream. You can also use any other booze that contains chocolate or vanilla flavor.

Special Tools and Utensils:

Use a food grade pastry brush

If you want to make the body paint into a unique gift, pick up some decorative jars for bottling up the chocolate body paint. This makes a very unique gift surprise!

Some Naughty Tips:

These brushes are available on Amazon.com, or your local drug store, or your local grocery store, or your local bake shop.

You can also find some very nice and decorative jars on sites like Amazon.com or personalize your own on sites like Zazzle.com and Cafepress.com.

This recipe makes 1/2 cup of chocolate body paint. Please triple the recipe to make the body paint as a gift for a friend. You can fill the chocolate body paint in a nice looking jar and it will be a very unique, personal, and unforgettable gift.

You can even go to a place called Cafepress.com and personalize your own jars. All you need is a

love themed sexy label that says something like: "For my naughty Friend". You can also only print his or her name on the logo and add the love date next to the name. You can get very creative with these sayings and quotes. I love to search the internet for the most unique and sexy quotes that I can come up with. Funny and naughty sayings always work best because they create the best emotional engaging effect!

Some More Naughty Gift Ideas:

For an extra special gift you can also go ahead and write your 2 names in gold letters. You can write the name of your lover and your own name above and below the words "Dessert's On Me!" Let your appetite run free with You as the dessert special. How can your lover resist this delicious treat?

You can wrap the glass jar with the body paint "treat" nestled in shredded red parchment and tied with an over the top raffia ribbon and give it to your lover as a gift!

This is a truly naughty, sexy, and very personal gift for your sweetheart!

Once it is unwrapped, put it in the microwave and heat it up to 98.6 degrees, test the paint first to prevent any burns. If the temperature is perfect, you can start applying the chocolate body paint liberally on your body and let your appetite run wild...you might serve some ice cold chocolate martinis while you are experiencing a hot chocolate body paint moment!

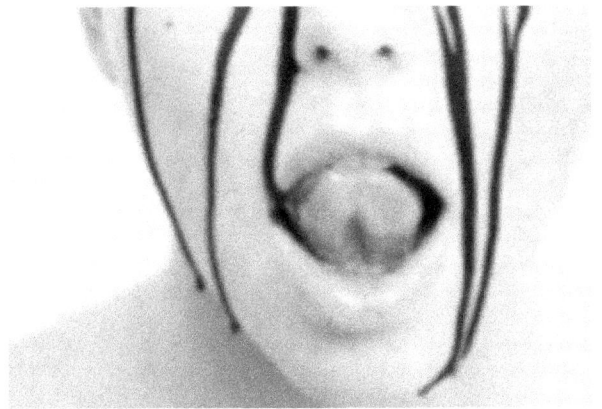

CAUTION

Please take precautions before painting the chocolate body paint on the body. Do not use the chocolate body paint until it has cooled down sufficiently. If the chocolate body paint is still too hot, you may get burned. Test a small drop of the paint first on your skin before liberally using the chocolate body paint.

Naughty Chocolate Body Paint Quiz

```
Naughty Chocolate Body Paint
D E L I C I O U S L
C W W Q Y X E S S O
N O I S S A P X J N
M M E S F H N A M C
V A O U W O E M J O
E N Y T H G U A N K
R U H O E R L S R M
C H O C O L A T E T
F R R E D B L O V E
C D G V Q Y J F Q M
        Paint Quiz
```

Here is another naughty and mentally stimulating activity for you that you can add to your love celebration. If you love to solve quizzes, you might like to solve the Naughty Chocolate Body Paint Quiz for yourself or with your lover to add some more emotionally stimulating moments. You can also turn this into a very naughty quiz game night with your lover!

Do not limit your creativity because the quiz is just another fun and inspirational game idea to think about. There are literally hundreds of other unique and creative ways how to add some other hot and sizzling naughty moments that are inspirational and mentally challenging.

Activities like games and quizzes are perfect to add to a Chocolate body paint session because you can even use this quiz as the creative inspiration for the body paint session that is coming up.

The quiz is also a good starter for a naughty night of games because it acts like a mental jugger!

So let's get started...

Instructions:

1. Use some paper to write down your quiz answers.

2. Hint: The correct answers are 10 words that relate to a very naughty love theme.

3. You and your partner can write down your 10 answers on the paper.

4. Check for the correct answers.

5. The winner must be rewarded at the end.

6. You can set your reward at the beginning and the winner who has found out all the correct answers is going to receive a nice reward. Here are some ideas: a massage, or he/she can choose who chocolate body paints the other, or he/she can set the rules for the rest of the evening, etc.

7. You can find lots of ideas for sexy rewards online. just do a quick research.

8. Add some other naughty games because this quiz is only meant to juggle more creative St Valentine activities and ideas that you can enjoy throughout your night of naughtiness!

9. Good luck with this naughty quiz.

Or you can add some sizzle like this...

Turning the Quiz into a Naughty Chocolate Body Paint Quiz Experience

Instead of thinking about some things that I can pain, I love to do this. I always like to come up with these quizzes in advance and instead of paper me and my partner write the answers of the quiz on our bodies.

Writing the answers with the body paint is much more sensual and emotionally engaging than using plain old paper and a pen. Use your bodies as the answer sheets and turn the body paint session into a naughty chocolate body paint quiz experience!

And One Last Thing

Always have an iced chocolate martini at your hands or your favorite cocktail because the warm body paint and the cool booze is going to be a sensational mix of emotions!

Answers
1. Love
2. Naughty
3. Chocolate
4. Delicious
5. Sexy
6. Heart
7. Red
8. Passion
9. Man
10. Woman

About the Publisher

InfinitYou is a hybrid general interest trade publisher. One of the first of its kind InfinitYou publishes physical books, electronic books, and audiobooks in various genres. Our publications are meant to educate, edify and entertain readers of all walks of life from babies to the elderly.

Home to more than twenty imprints such as Infinit Baby, Infinit Kids, Infinit Girl, Infinit Boy, Infinit Coloring, Infinit Swear Words, Infinit Activities, Infinit Productivity, Infinit Cat, Infinit Dog, Infinit Love, Infinit Family, Infinit Survival, Infinit Health, Infinit Beauty, Infinit Spirituality, Infinit Lifestyle, Infinit Wealth, Infinit Romance, and lots more.

www.ingramcontent.com/pod-product-compliance
Lightning Source LLC
LaVergne TN
LVHW020509080526
838202LV00057B/6270